My Life Cycle

My Life as a
GREAT WHITE
SHARK

PICTURE WINDOW BOOKS
a capstone imprint

Published by Picture Window Books, an imprint of Capstone
1710 Roe Crest Drive, North Mankato, Minnesota 56003
capstonepub.com

Library of Congress Cataloging-in-Publication Data
Names: Sazaklis, John, author. | Pang, Bonnie, illustrator.
Title: My life as a great white shark / by John Sazaklis ; illustrated by Bonnie Pang.
Description: North Mankato : Picture Window Books, an imprint of Capstone,
[2022] | Series: My life cycle | Includes bibliographical references and index. |
Audience: Ages 5-7 | Audience: Grades K-1 | Summary: "Hi, there! I'm a great
white shark. Don't let my sharp teeth scare you off. I started life much smaller, just
like you! Learn more about my life cycle and how I went from a tiny little shark
pup to the ocean's top predator."—Provided by publisher.
Identifiers: LCCN 2021019167 (print) | LCCN 2021019168 (ebook) |
  ISBN 9781663984852 (hardcover) | ISBN 9781666332834 (pdf) |
  ISBN 9781666332858 (kindle edition)
Subjects: LCSH: White shark—Life cycles—Juvenile literature.
Classification: LCC QL638.95.L3 S29 2022 (print) | LCC QL638.95.L3 (ebook) |
DDC 597.3/3156—dc23
LC record available at https://lccn.loc.gov/2021019167
LC ebook record available at https://lccn.loc.gov/2021019168

Editorial Credits
Editor: Alison Deering; Designer: Kay Fraser; Media Researcher: Svetlana Zhurkin;
Production Specialist: Katy LaVigne

Printed in the United States   5087

My Life as a
GREAT WHITE
SHARK

by John Sazaklis

illustrated by Bonnie Pang

GRRRR! I am a great white shark! I am large and in charge!

Scientists try their best to study great white sharks, but we like to be mysterious. We got our name because of our pale, white underbellies.

Lucky for you, I'm willing to give you the inside scoop on my life in the ocean!

Let's start with size—they don't call me *great* for nothing.
I am the ruler of the ocean!

Believe it or not, I wasn't always big. I started off as
a teeny tiny egg that could fit in the palm of your hand!

Because I was so tiny, I had to share my space.
My mom carried me in an egg pouch in her belly
with about five other eggs.

The future ruler of the ocean having roommates?
How rude!

If that wasn't bad enough, I had to eat the other eggs while I was in my mom's belly! She made extra for me to snack on.

I also had to swallow my own teeth. They gave me the **calcium** and **minerals** I needed to grow, but YUCK!

No biggie, though. I have about 300 chompers. If I lose or break any, I just pop out a few more from the seven rows of backups in my mouth. (If you count those, I can have up to 3,000 teeth at once!)

After about 14 months inside the egg pouch, my siblings and I are roughly 4 to 5 feet (1.2 to 1.5 meters) long. Time to hatch! Ah, sweet freedom! No more sharing an itty-bitty living space with five other **pups**.

Baby sharks are not the cute, furry kind of pups that bark and roll over. We're pups with fins and **gills** and a tail.

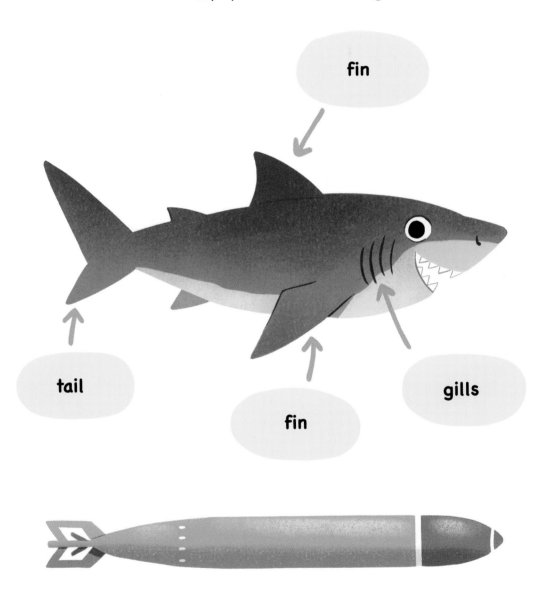

Does my tail wag when I'm happy? Don't be ridiculous! It zooms me forward like a turbo **torpedo**!

No self-respecting great white shark needs swim lessons, thank you very much. I learned to swim on my own. I'm a natural! No floaties or life vest needed for me.

A shark needs its own space, and I'm ready for some **independence**. I take off for the great, wide ocean.

See ya! Wouldn't wanna be ya!

I was also born a natural hunter. Aside from terrific teeth, I also have taste buds inside my mouth and throat. They help me find food.

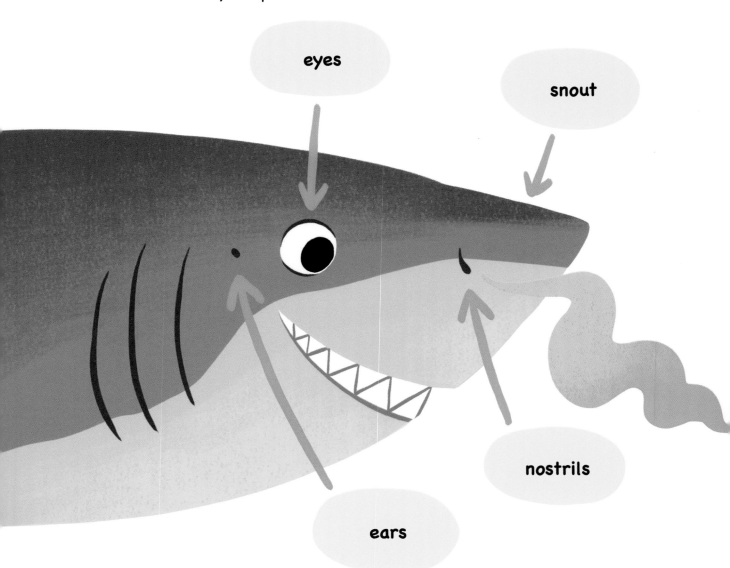

eyes

snout

nostrils

ears

What other wonderful features do I have? Why, thank you for asking. I have a pair of nostrils on the underside of my snout. SNIFF, SNIFF!

I also have deep dark blue eyes with super vision and tiny little ears that you can't see. Can you imagine a creature with ears sticking out of its head? How silly that would be!

I use my super senses to watch out for hungry creatures, like dolphins or whales. They might make a meal out of shark pups like me. Bigger sharks want me for a snack too!

Speaking of eating, I'm starving! Small fish and **stingrays** are on the mini menu for a shark pup. MMMM!

Young sharks grow *very* slowly. It takes boys almost 10 years to grow into adults. It takes girls even longer! They're not adults until 12 to 14 years old.

YOUNG OF THE YEAR

During that time, we get stronger and faster. I can swim as fast as 35 miles (56 kilometers) per hour and dive as deep as 3,900 feet (1,189 m)!

I don't want to brag, but I'm kind of a big deal! But not quite big enough to be at the top of the **food chain**. . . .

I keep growing and eating and *growing*. By the time I'm an adult, I measure up to 20 feet (6.1 m) long and weigh as much as 5,000 pounds (2,268 kilograms). Must be all that water weight. Ha ha!

Did you know female great whites are bigger and stronger than males? Talk about girl power!

The only animal higher than me on the food chain is the orca—also known as the killer whale. With a name like that, it might try to eat me as a snack. Better watch out!

Speaking of *big* things, I now have an **appetite** the size of my body. In one year alone, I can eat 11 tons (9,979 kg) of food.

May I see the menu for mega munchers, please?
Ah, yes—this is more like it. Look at all the tasty treats!
Those dolphins better watch out. It's payback time!

My love for food takes me around the globe. I follow my nose to places with lots of fish and sea **mammals**.

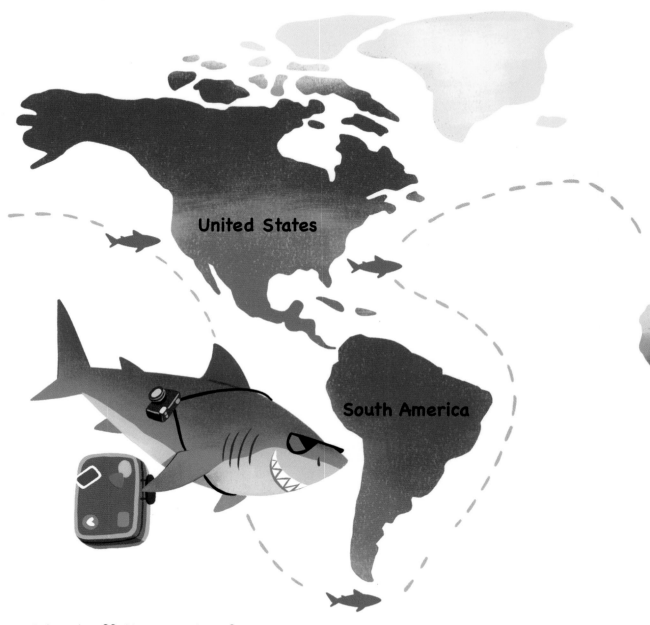

I hunt off the coasts of the United States, South America, Japan, Australia, New Zealand, and Africa. I even visit the Mediterranean for some fun in the sun.

And since I plan on living for 60 years—maybe more!—I can visit these places over and over again. I'm a regular world traveler!

Japan

Africa

Australia

New Zealand

If you think you'd like to meet me on my travels, you're not alone. Humans try to study and watch me inside underwater cages. They even make books and movies about me.

I'm really flattered, but the best (and safest) way to learn my secrets is to pick up a *fin-tastic* book—like this one!—and dive right in!

My Life as a Great White Shark

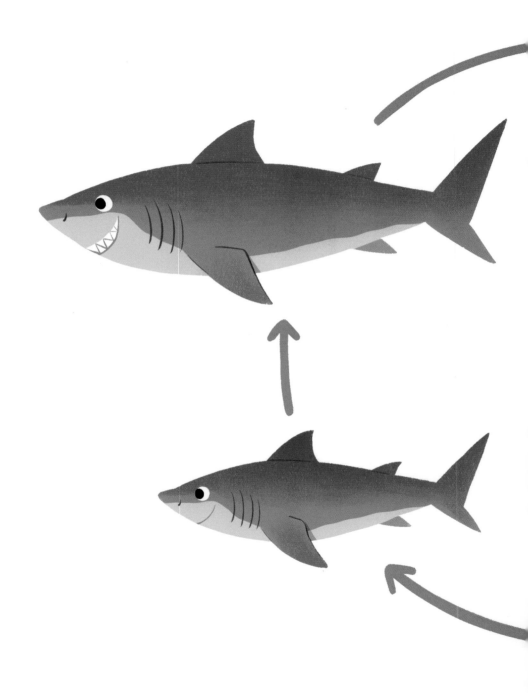

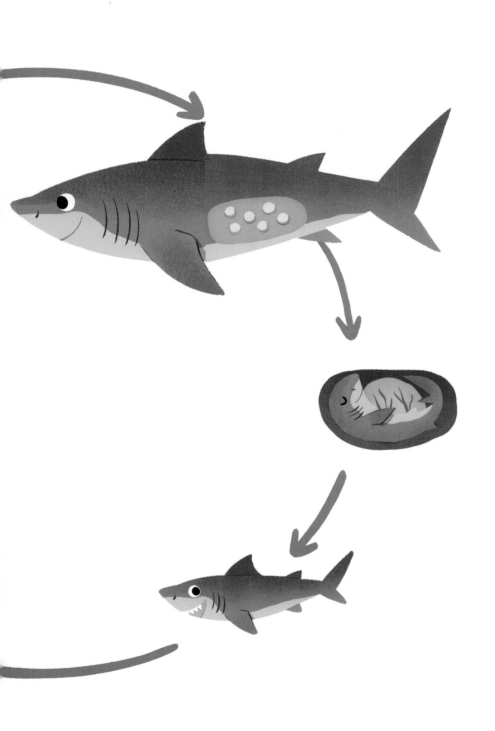

About the Author

John Sazaklis is a *New York Times* bestselling author with more than 100 children's books under his utility belt! He has also illustrated Spider-Man books, created toys for *MAD* magazine, and written for the *BEN 10* animated series. John lives in New York City with his superpowered wife and daughter.

About the Illustrator

Bonnie Pang is an illustrator and comic artist from Hong Kong. She currently illustrates children's books and creates the webcomic *IT Guy & ART Girl*. When not drawing, she enjoys watching movies, gardening, and exploring new places.

Glossary

appetite (AP-uh-tite)—a desire for food or drink

calcium (KAL-see-uhm)—a soft, silver-white mineral found in teeth and bones

food chain (FOOD CHAYN)—a series of types of living things in which each one uses the next lower member of the chain as a source of food

gill (GIL)—a body part on the side of a fish or shark used to breathe underwater

independence (in-di-PEN-duhnss)—freedom

mammal (MAM-uhl)—a warm-blooded animal that breathes air; mammals have hair or fur; female mammals feed milk to their young

mineral (MIN-ur-uhl)—a material found in nature that is not an animal or a plant

pup (PUHP)—a young shark

stingray (STING-rey)—a fish that has a flat body, fins that look like wings, and a long, poisonous tail

torpedo (tor-PEE-doh)—a very fast underwater missile

Index